WØØØ9Ø77

A special thanks to:

Beef photos courtesy of the
National Cattlemen's Beef Association
444 North Michigan Avenue/Suite 1800, Chicago, IL 60611-9909

Pork photos courtesy of
National Pork Producers Council
P.O. Box 10383, Des Moines, IA 50306

Chicken photos courtesy of
National Chicken Council
1015 15th Street NW, Suite 930, Washington, D.C. 20005-2622

CONTENTS

Appendix – Additional Articles and Recipes

    Talking Turkey

    What To Do with the Leftover Turkey

    John's Very Own Turkey Enchiladas

    Turkey Pot Pie "Bachelor Style"

    Totally Awesome Chili

    John's Awesome Way Good Cheap Chili

    Cheap and Easy Meat Loaf

    Marine Corps Railroad-Style Barbecue Sauce

    Way Easy and Way Delectable Ribs

    Tools of the Trade

    Butcher Etiquette

THE CONFESSION

It's early in the morning. The sun is still hours from rising, and the day's mischief is being planned. There will be hundreds of people coming through the doors with money in their pockets, and it is our job to separate them from as much of it as possible. There is nothing new to what we do. Our skills of legal larceny have been handed down through several generations, and with each generation comes a more refined and sophisticated approach to what we like to call "merchandising."

A cutting list is made, and the traps are soon in place. The meat aisle quickly fills with consumers. They walk up and down the meat case bewildered and confused. They sometimes ask the butcher for help and, with a smile, he swiftly guides them to a profit spot. Or they strike out on their own in their confused state and make a selection. Either way, they're ours. We've got them right where we want them.

We are not bad guys—most of us are quite friendly and approachable. We try to help you find what you want, but the merchandising schemes are so entrenched that we don't even recognize the larceny in our own actions. In fact, butchers often fall into their own traps. Many times I have seen a fellow meat cutter pay the full amount for an overpriced, overmerchandised cut of meat when, if he would have given it some thought, he could have come up with an alternative for a lot less money. There is no need to spend the kind of money for meat that most of us do.

In the early days of the retail meat markets, there were only a few basic cuts of meat. Now there are hundreds. Where have they come from? When we merchandise a cut of meat, it means we cut it into as many different shapes and sizes as we possibly can. Then we convince you, the consumer, that you need just this cut of meat in just these proportions and dimensions for the dish you are preparing. Nothing else will do! Of course, it's gonna cost ya! Hee! Hee! Oh what fun we have had—at your expense, of course.

After 31 years of fleecing the public, I wish to come clean. In this book, I will expose virtually every merchandising scheme in the retail meat industry. I will show you, the consumer, how to circumvent the merchandising traps. I will show you how to get that quality cut of meat you want, for your specific application, for a lot less money.

Please Note:

You will find that I have not attempted to list prices of any retail cuts of meat. For me to do so would be confusing and inaccurate at best, since each part of the country is different and prices fluctuate from day to day as well. For example, in California tri-tip roasts are a popular barbecue item. Since they are popular with

California's perennial barbecuers, the supermarkets may use them in their ads to lure customers. They may mark them way down. On the other hand, in the western portion of Oregon, where it rains all the time, people are not demanding tri-tips for their barbecue grill (which is out in the garage buried under camping gear and the like most of the year). So the meat departments sell them, for the most part, at a premium to the few who want them. What I try and do is show you the many options for each cut of meat, directing you to ones that will save you money.

Another Note:

Purchase every option that I list on sale, whenever possible, to ensure that you are taking maximum advantage of what is available in terms of savings.

A Few Words About Merchandising

In the old days, the fatted calf was butchered and hung to cool and age. Then it was divided into a few primal cuts. A primal cut is a main section of the carcass such as the chuck, round, loin, etc. The butchers would take each primal and cut some of it thin for steaks, cut some of it in chunks for roasts, and use the trim that was left over for stew meat or hamburger. Pretty simple. So why are there so many different cuts of beef in your average supermarket meat case? Merchandising, that's why!

The butchers of old would simply grab a short loin (the primal where T-bone steaks come from) and cut T-bone steaks and price them all the same. Then some overachieving butcher came up with the bright idea of calling the first four steaks off the short loin porterhouses instead of T-bones and charging more for them. That worked out pretty well. Then someone else (or maybe it was the same guy, I don't know) thought folks might like a boneless T-bone steak that wasn't so darned big. So he removed the bone from the short loin. Now you have loin strip steak (New York) and tenderloin (filet mignon). Of course, these steaks will cost you quite a bit of money. Next thing you know, butchers everywhere were trying to outdo one another with their merchandising of those few primals until most folks didn't know what was what.

Now, the one thing consumers do know is that they had better bring plenty of money with them to the local supermarket if they plan on purchasing meat.

In this section, I will show you all the different cuts of beef and how you can get them or an alternative of equal or better quality for less money (sometimes a lot less money). The opposite of merchandise is demerchandise, and that is what I'm going to show you!

QUALITY STEAKS FOR BROILING OR GRILLING

Rib Eye:

Money-saving alternatives: prime rib, rib steaks, and chuck eye.

Rib eyes are wonderful little steaks, very tender and with lots of flavor. They are also very expensive. If you just have to have a rib eye, and I don't blame you if you do, but do not want to spend the money, no problem. The rib eye is the same cut of beef as the

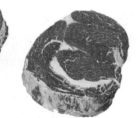

Beef Rib Eye Steak

prime rib or the rib steak but without the bone. Both the rib steak and the prime rib are quite a bit cheaper than the rib eye (often two to three dollars a pound cheaper). Purchase whichever is cheaper. If the prime rib is the cheapest, ask the butcher to cut it into steaks for you.

An even cheaper substitute for the rib eye is the chuck eye. The eye of the chuck is basically the same cut of beef as the rib eye. The rib eye extends from the loin up into the first six inches or so of the chuck and makes outstanding little steaks. They are a little bit smaller than the rib eye and may have a little more fat, but for my money it's the way to go. Watch for boneless chucks on sale and you will find the meat case full of chuck eyes, hopefully priced to sell. If you want a really good deal, ask the butcher to cut off the first four to six inches of a boneless chuck next time boneless chuck roasts are one sale. Then ask the butcher to peel out the eye and cut it into steaks. Use the trim for stew meat or have the butcher grind it into hamburger, or take it all home and do it yourself. You have just saved a bundle.

Top Sirloin:

Money-saving alternatives: whole top sirloins "in the bag," if priced right, and petite sirloins.

Top sirloins make nice lean and tender steaks. They are often on sale at reasonable prices. However, you can find whole top sirloins "in the bag" even cheaper. "In the bag" means the meat is still in the vacuum-sealed package from the wholesale processor. Some of them are trimmed and some are not. A whole top sirloin "in the bag" can have up to two inches of fat cover as well as gristly end pieces. The whole top must be pretrimmed and at least one dollar a pound less than the down-and-dirty, rock-bottom sale price of the steaks or it is not worth it.

Petite sirloins are nothing more than a glorified sirloin tip steak off the round. Having said that, they are not a bad little steak to broil or throw on the barbecue. They are often on sale for less than the top sirloin steaks.

Chateaubriand:

Money-saving alternatives: thick-cut top sirloin steak, thick-cut top round, London broil.

Watch out for Chateaubriand! In most stores, it is nothing more than a thick-cut top sirloin steak (a true Chateau is a butt tenderloin) and is sometimes priced higher to take advantage of the unsuspecting consumer. If you wish to have a nice juicy chateau for dinner and your local retail meat seller jacks up the price, then simply ask for a thick (two- to three-inch) top sirloin steak. If he insists on calling it a Chateau and charges you extra, then go somewhere else.

London broil, a thick-cut top-round steak, can be prepared just as you would a Chateaubriand, with similar results. The London broil, or top-round steak or roast, has a reputation as a tough cut of beef. However, if you broil or grill the London broil until it is medium rare to medium (never overcook it), then slice it thin across the grain and serve it, it will be nice and juicy and tender. Top-round London broil can be found on sale cheap and often.

T-Bone:

Money-saving alternative: New York steaks on sale.

A T-bone is a T-bone is a T-bone, and there are no alternatives unless you don't mind purchasing just the New York portion. The T-bone steak is two steaks in one. There is the New York steak on the top or outside portion and the tenderloin (filet) on the bottom or the inside portion, and they are separated by a T-shaped bone. Look for T-bone steaks on sale,

T-Bone Steak

or you can often find a boneless New York steak on sale for even less, sometimes a lot less, and you will not have to throw away a bone that cost you good money.

Filet Mignon (Tenderloin):

Money-saving alternative: Split a thick juicy T-bone steak with someone, the New York for your loved one and the filet for you.

Beef tenderloin in the bag can be several dollars cheaper than the already trimmed filets in the meat case. There is some trim loss, but you should save some money. Ask the butcher for a whole butt tender still in the bag and then ask him to cut it into steaks.

New York (Loin Strip):

Money-saving alternatives: small end rib steak, T-bone if the ad is hot ($1 a pound less than the normal ad price of a New York steak or forget it).

The loin or the "back strap," as the deer hunters like to call it, extends through the rib and into the first few inches of the chuck. The loin becomes a little more rounded and a little more marbled (flecks of fat) as it makes its way through the rib but is essentially the same cut of beef. So if you are looking for a nice New York steak, the first few cuts of the rib (rib steak or rib eye) are very

Boneless Top Loin Strip Steak (New York Steak)

similar and are often less money than the New York. The only real difference between the New York and the first few cuts of the rib is the rib steak has a small rib bone. If rib steaks are on sale and New Yorks are not, look for a nice lean rib steak and you will be happy!

Rib Steak:

Money-saving alternatives: if on sale, New York steak, prime rib, chuck eye.

Rib steaks are delicious. They have a little more marbling than the other "good" steaks, which gives them superior flavor and juiciness. Sometimes New York steaks are on sale for less than the rib steak. The rib end of the New York is practically the same as a rib steak. Look for the New York steaks that are full and more rounded, not slender. Prime rib is the same cut of beef as the rib steak, only thicker. If prime ribs are on sale for less than rib steaks, grab one and ask the butcher to cut it into steaks for you. The chuck eye is the same cut of beef as the rib, only it becomes more rounded and more marbled as it extends into the chuck. If you want a good steak cheap, the chuck eye is the way to go. To really save money, wait until boneless chucks are on sale. Ask the butcher for the first four inches off the boneless chuck. Then ask him to peel out the eye and cut it into steaks. Grind or make stew meat out of what is left. You now have really good steaks at hamburger prices.

Beef Rib Steak

London Broil:

Money-saving alternatives: when on sale, baron of beef (thick round steak), top-round roast, watermelon-cut rump roast.

Next time you're looking for a London broil, check the ads and see who has round steaks on sale. Better yet, do not wait until you want a London broil. As soon as you see a really hot round steak ad, ask the butcher for about a three-inch-thick round steak. Also ask him to separate the top, bottom, and eye. You can have him cut the eye and the bottom into steaks, stir fry, stew meat, cube steaks, or hamburger while keeping the top for a London broil. Then throw it all in the freezer. If you want to stock up, ask for a six-inch-thick round steak. Then the butcher can cut you two London broils, the eye, and the bottom into roasts or any combination of cuts as before. Top-round steaks are sometimes on sale for less than London broil. Ask the butcher for a two- to three-inch top-round steak. The watermelon rump roast is the top-round portion of the rump. It can be used as a London broil. It is shaped a little funny, but you can fix that. If rumps are on sale, ask for a four-inch-thick watermelon cut and then take it home and simply trim off the rounded side to make it flat. Use the trim for stew or something and the rest as a London broil. Be careful though, because some of the young meat cutters may not know what a watermelon cut is and might try and slip you a bottom round roast.

Porterhouse:

Money-saving alternative: T-bone.

The porterhouse steak is nothing more than one of the first three or four T-bone steaks cut off the large end of the short loin.

The first T-bones are larger with larger tenderloins (filets) and New York. As you cut through the short loin, the filets get smaller as do the New Yorks, to some degree. But it is all the same meat. The T-bone steak will be just as tasty as the porterhouse. But if you want a great big T-bone with a large filet, the porterhouse is the steak for you. But don't pay the extra money the butcher may charge for the porters. Many meat markets label and price the porterhouse as T-bones, so just look for the large T-bones and save yourself a little money.

Flank Steak:

Money-saving alternative: for broiled or grilled flank steak, none; the flank is very unique with a nice texture and flavor. For some recipes a top round steak may work, see below.

For stuffed flank steak, you can substitute a top-round steak. It does not have quite the same texture as the flank, and it will probably turn out on the dry side, but it will work and be much cheaper. A lot of recipes call for thin-sliced top-round for stuffing. Look for top-round London broil on sale or top-round roast and ask the butcher to slice it about three quarters of an inch thick and run it through the tenderizer (if your recipe calls for it).

Flank Steak

Petite Sirloin:

Money-saving alternatives: top sirloin, sirloin tip, top blade (flatiron).

Petite sirloins are a relatively new steak, at least around these parts. The first time I saw a petite sirloin was about 1990. People seem to like them because they are lean, fairly tender, and small. They are cut from somewhere off or partly next to the sirloin tip (another good example of merchandising). The sirloin tip, which is not really a sirloin but part of the round, is a decent steak. If marinated and grilled to just the right medium rareness, the tip steak can be upgraded to "pretty darn good." You can find either the sirloin tip (round tip steak) or the petite sirloin on sale at decent prices. Buy the cheapest. Be careful, though. A lot of meat cutters don't bother to cut the sirloin tip across the grain, which can make a big difference in chewability. Top sirloin steaks are often on sale cheaper than either the tip or the petite and are a quality lean steak that doesn't need marinating. Go with the top sirloin as long as the price is similar. If you don't mind a little more marbling, you can find the top blade or flatiron for less money than most steaks, and it is very good.

Tri-Tip Roast or Steak:

Money-saving alternatives: flatiron, boneless chuck flat strips.

The tri-tip is a unique cut of beef. Merchandised off of the hindquarter, the tri-tip is a very good barbecue item, as are the steaks. They are fairly tender, with nice marbling (flecks of fat), which makes them juicy and flavorful. There is only one cut of beef that I consider some-

Tri-Tip Roast

what similar to the tri-tip roast and that is the flatiron and maybe the chuck flat strip. I guess that's two cuts that are similar to the tri-tip. Anyhow, the flatiron is cut from the cross rib and is usually reserved for making boneless country-style ribs and top-blade steaks or roasts (see top-blade roasts). Ask the butcher how much a flat-iron roast is going for. You can often get a flatiron much cheaper than a tri-tip. It isn't very pretty, but it will cook up as either a roast or steaks in much the same way as the tri-tip. In fact, I prefer the flatiron over almost all other cuts except maybe a rib eye. But if it means the difference of three or four dollars a pound, I'm going with the flatiron every time. Also, the boneless chuck flat strip will eat very similar to the tri-tip steak or roast and for a lot less money. Give either one of them a try and save.

Sirloin Tip or Round-Tip Steak:

Money-saving alternatives: top sirloin, petite sirloin, tri-tip steak; possibly rib steak, T-bone steak, or New York steak if on sale; top blade chuck steak (flatiron).

The sirloin tip steak, also called a round-tip steak, is a very lean marginal broil or grilling steak and is generally overpriced. If marinated, it can be pretty good. The top sirloin is a better steak, and can often be found cheaper than the sirloin tip. If you buy petite sirloin it is basically the same cut of beef as the sirloin tip steak and at times is cheaper as well. The tri-tip steak, which is not as lean, is sometimes cheaper than the sirloin tip and will have more flavor with similar tenderness. Also, the flatiron, which has good marbling, will be cheaper than the tip steak almost every day of the week and is a far better piece of meat. Sometimes, if you watch the ads you can find some of the better steaks such as T-bones, rib steaks, and New Yorks cheaper than the tip steaks at regular price. If you do, go for them instead.

Chuck Eye Steak:

Money-saving alternatives: top blade steak (flatiron), chuck flat strips, boneless chuck roast.

The boneless chuck eye is a very nice steak. It is actually part of the same muscle as the rib eye. It just gets a little smaller and more marbled as it extends into the chuck. When boneless chuck roasts are on sale, ask the butcher for a nice four-inch chuck and have him peel out the eye and cut it into steaks. Then use the rest for stew or grind it up for hamburger. You have just saved a bundle. Or, ask for a couple of flatiron steaks. They are usually reasonably priced and are very good. The chuck flat strip can be cut into steak dimensions and is quite juicy and flavorful and will chew up ok if you still possess most of your teeth. Go with whichever is cheaper.

Top Blade Steak (Flatiron):

Money-saving alternatives: boneless chuck eye, boneless chuck flat strip.

First just let me say that the flatiron is the most underrated piece of meat in the counter. It is tender, flavorful and cheap. Most of the time, the flatiron will be sold as a boneless beef country style rib. Ask the butcher if you can't find them. A very nice alternative to the flatiron steak is the boneless chuck flat strip. It is usually sold as boneless beef ribs but is very similar to the flatiron in juiciness, flavor, and

Top Blade or Flatiron Steaks

tenderness. It is very good grilled medium rare to medium, and I just love it. The price is right as well. A boneless chuck eye is a good alternative too. If you buy the first 4-to-6 inches of a boneless chuck roast on sale and peel out the eye and use the rest for stew meat or hamburger, you can save a bundle.

STEAKS FOR SWISSING AND TENDERIZING

Beef Steaks for Swissing are generally steaks that are not very tender unless they are cooked slowly in moist heat. They can be tenderized with a mallet, or the butcher can run them through his tenderizer a couple of times. They are now called cubed steaks. Flour them up and fry them in hot grease for chicken fried steak.

Boneless Chuck Steak:

Money-saving alternative: when chuck steaks are on sale, there is no cheaper alternative.

There is nothing cheaper than a boneless chuck steak when it is on sale, except maybe a bone-in chuck steak on sale. The chuck steaks make very good Swiss steaks and, when marinated, can be barbecued as well. Of course, chuck steaks aren't always on sale, and when they are not and you want a steak for swissing, there are alternatives. A rump roast or a cross rib roast, if on sale, will make outstanding Swiss steaks. Pick out a roast that is priced right from the meat case and ask the butcher to slice it into steaks. Also ask the butcher about flatirons. They make very good Swiss steaks with excellent flavor and are often found reasonably priced.

Bottom Round Steak:

Money-saving alternatives: round steak, top-round London broil, rump roast, and cross rib roast.

Almost any slice of meat will work in replacing the bottom round steak for either tenderizing for chicken fried steak or for Swissing. To save money, have the rump roast, cross rib roast, top-round London broil, or round steak, on sale, cut into portion-sized steaks for either Swissing or chicken fry in place of the bottom round steak.

Cross Rib Steak or Ranch Steak:

Money-saving alternatives: cross rib roast, rump roast, top-round London broil, and round steak.

The cross rib steak is a great steak for Swissing or for marinating. It can be chewy but has great flavor. The only real problem with the cross rib steak is that it is usually way overpriced. Grab one of the cross rib roasts from the counter and ask the butcher to cut it into steaks for you the next time it is on sale at an irresistible price. The top-round London broil, top-round steak or roast, as well as a full-cut round steak make great Swiss or tenderized steaks for chicken fry as well. Go with whatever is cheapest, and ask the butcher to cut it up and tenderize it, if desired.

Top-Round Steak:

Money-saving alternatives: top-round London broil, full-cut round steak, rump roast.

Top-round steaks are great for Swissing and make outstanding chicken fried steaks. You can even marinate them for a somewhat decent broil or barbecue steak. However, they are usually overpriced. The London broil is the same cut as the top round but thicker and usually cheaper and can be cut into steaks for Swissing or chicken fry. Round steaks or rump roasts are often on sale even cheaper than the London broil. Have the butcher cut them into portion-sized steaks for you instead of the top-round steak.

Mock Tender:

Money-saving alternatives: rump roast, cross rib roast.

The mock tender is round and lean and looks something like a filet but eats more like a hockey puck. Of course, marinating can help, as does Swissing or running it through a tenderizer machine. The mock tender is usually priced to sell, but a cross rib roast, rump roast, or top-round roast may be cheaper and will work as well as the mock for the same applications.

Eye of Round Steak:

Money-saving alternative: Almost every cut of beef is cheaper and better than this grossly overpriced and overrated cut.

The eye of round is lean and pretty and you get more chew for the dollar than any other cut unless you marinate, Swiss, or have the butcher run it through the tenderizer. If you do one or more of these things, then the eye is a pretty darn good steak but not as good as the price tag often suggests. Cut a rump roast, top-round roast, London broil, or full-cut round steak into portion-sized steaks. Any of these suggestions will save you money unless the eye of round steaks are on sale. Just go with whichever is cheaper.

Full-Cut Round Steak:

Money-saving alternative: When round steaks are on sale, they are hard to beat.

Full-cut round steak is an excellent Swiss steak. It is also used to make cube steaks for chicken fry, lean strips for stir fry, stew meat, hamburger, and when cut thick, roasts. It is often on sale at bottom-dollar

Full-Cut Round Steak

prices as a leader item to get the shopper into the store.

On sale it is a great value, one that is hard to beat. But sometimes you can find rump roasts (rump roasts are nothing more than a chunk of the round instead of a slice) cheaper than round steaks. When this happens, ask the butcher to cut a rump roast into Swiss or cube steaks or whatever you were going to use the round steak for.

ROASTS

Rump Roast Boneless:

Money-saving alternatives: when on sale, thick-cut round steak, top-round roast, London broil, bottom-round roast, cross rib roast.

The true rump roast is the chunk that is cut off the end of the round to square it up before cutting full round steaks. The rump is three cuts in one and is usually divided into three separate roasts. There is the bottom-round portion, the top-round portion (watermelon cut), and the eye of round or the three-in-one portion (it has a little bit of all three cuts). Any one of these roasts will make an excellent oven roast. Sometimes the top-round roast or London broil is on sale for less than the rump. If the Londons are on sale, ask the butcher to cut a six-inch London broil and then cut it in two. You now have two approximately three-and-a half-pound top-round roasts. Now, if full-cut round steaks are this week's leader item at your local supermarket and you want a rump roast for dinner or you want to fill your freezer and save lots of money, you're in luck. Go to the store and ask the butcher for a six- to ten-inch-thick round steak. If you are on good terms with your butcher, ask him to cut it into roasts for you or you can take it home and cut it into whatever size chunks you want. You can also make stew meat, cube steaks, Swiss steaks, stir fry, ground round, jerky meat, fajita meat, or whatever your creative mind can think of out of thick-cut round steaks on sale and save money to boot!

Bottom-Round Roast:

Money-saving alternatives: rump roasts or, if on sale, top-round roasts, London broils, thick-cut round steak, cross rib roast.

Bottom Round Roast

Usually the bottom-round roast is marked as a rump roast in the meat case. If you ask for a bottom-round roast, you may be charged more, so don't. Just look for the best deal on any oven roast. Top-round London broils make great oven roasts (if they are cut thick enough), as do rumps and cross ribs. A round steak on sale, cut thick and then divided into roasts, is usually the least expensive way to go when looking for a nice oven roast.

Top-Round Roast:

Money-saving alternatives: rump roast, top-round London broil, thick-cut round steak, cross rib roast.

The rump roast is often on sale for less than what you would pay for a top-round roast and is very similar. Also, the top-round London broil is often on sale and is nothing more than a thick top-round steak. Ask the butcher to cut you an extra-thick London if it is on sale and then cut it in half into roasts, one for now and one for the freezer. Or, if round steaks are on sale, ask for a thick (at least five inches) round steak and make roasts from the top round portion. The rest can be cut into eye of round steaks, bottom round steaks, cube steaks, stew meat, stir fry, ground beef, or more roasts.

Eye of Round Roast:

Money-saving alternatives: top-round roast or London broil, sirloin (round) tip roast, top sirloin roast.

The eye of round is a dandy little roast, great for French dip. However it is usually way overpriced. A nice rump, top-round, or sirloin tip roast is often a better value. If you just have to have the eye of round, look for full-cut round steaks on sale. When you find them, ask the butcher for a four- to ten-inch-thick round steak, and have him peel out the eye for a roast. The rest of the thick-cut round steak may be used for steaks, roasts, hamburger, stew, stir fry, etc. Top sirloin roast isn't much like an eye of round, but if you're going to pay regular price for an eye, you might consider a top sirloin. They are nice and tender and are sometimes on sale lower than the eye of round. Watch for a top sirloin steak sale, and ask the butcher for a roast instead.

Baron of Beef:

Money-saving alternatives: rump roast, top-round London broil, round steak.

The baron of beef is a very thick (two inches or more) full-cut round steak. When round steaks are on sale, the barons should be the same price. If not, ask for a round steak cut thick to your specification. You will be getting a baron priced as a round steak. You have just outsmarted the butcher. Large rump roasts and very thick London broils are all in the same family and will eat the same. Go with whatever is cheaper.

Sirloin Tip Roast (Round Tip Roast):

Money-saving alternatives: rump roast or, when on sale, top-round roast, London broil, and top sirloin roast.

The sirloin or round tip roast is a very nice oven roast but so is the rump and the top-round roast or London broil. Go with whatever is cheaper. Look for a round steak ad, and have the butcher cut you a thick one (at least five inches) and have him divide it into roasts.

Sometimes top sirloin steaks are on sale for less than sirloin tip roasts. If this is the case, ask for a top sirloin roast. The top sirloin is of a higher quality than the sirloin tip. You might also look at top sirloins whole and "in the bag." Whole tops are priced lower than the steaks and will yield two or three very nice roasts. Be careful if the whole tops are untrimmed. You will be paying for the extra fat.

Note: When purchasing a sirloin tip roast, always ask for the silver or solid side.

Top Sirloin Roast:

Money-saving alternatives: top-round roast, sirloin (round) tip roast, rump roast.

The top sirloin can make a very nice oven roast but so does a rump, sirloin tip or top-round. Now if you have your mind made up and a top sirloin roast is what you want, look for top sirloins whole and "in the bag." They are occasionally on sale, but even when they are not they should be priced less than the steaks. Sometimes you will find them to be quite cheap. Just watch out for excessive fat covering the top. Also, whenever top sirloin steaks are on sale, you should be able to get a top sirloin roast for the same price. First, ask how much the whole tops in the bag are before making your purchase. Remember that you are paying for the fat, so make sure that the whole untrimmed top sirloins are at least one dollar a pound cheaper than the trimmed ones.

Prime Rib or Standing Rib:

Money-saving alternative: See below.

There is no other roast with the flavor, juiciness, or tenderness of the prime rib. You can save money by purchasing a nice rump, top-round, or top sirloin roast, but it just isn't the same. The only way to save money on a prime rib, if you are not willing to settle, is to wait until it is on sale. Watch for rib steaks in the ads too. Rib steaks are prime ribs sliced

Prime Rib Roast
Small End

to steak specifications. When they are on sale, you can usually get a prime rib for the same price. If the butcher does not want to give you a prime rib at the rib steak price, then firmly request a very thick rib steak. Four inches or more will make a very nice roast, and every one inch is approximately (loose approximation) one pound.

Chuck Roast Boneless:

Money-saving alternative: When boneless chucks are at their rock-bottom sale price, there is no cheaper alternative.

Sometimes the old seven-bone or blade chuck roasts are available cheap. But if you watch the ads, you will find that boneless chucks are sometimes just as cheap, or darn near and without the bone, making them the better value. One word of caution: Watch out for chuck roasts when they are not on sale. For some reason, many of the retailers are mighty proud of them and the price will reflect it. A nice cross rib roast on sale will probably be cheaper than a chuck roast that isn't and cooks up very good as a pot roast.

Seven-Bone & Blade Chuck Roast (Bone-In Chuck):

Money-saving alternative: boneless chuck roast.

There is so much bone, fat, and gristle in a bone-in chuck roast that it needs to be quite a bit cheaper than a boneless chuck to make it worthwhile. However, the bone-in chucks are sometimes on sale dirt cheap when boneless chucks are priced through the roof. If this is the case, by all means grab one for dinner. It makes a great pot roast. I just wouldn't stock up on them to save money. Chances are that boneless chuck roasts will be one sale somewhere soon at a very good price.

Arm or Round Bone Roast:

Money-saving alternatives: boneless chuck roast, cross rib roast.

In my humble opinion, this is the greatest of the pot roasts. They no longer exist in many retail markets because of the continuing evolution of meat merchandising. The cross rib roast is the meaty section of the arm and is a very good pot roast. On sale, the cross rib is a good value. Of all the pot roasts, boneless chuck roasts on sale will generally be the best deal.

Cross Rib Roast:

Money-saving alternative: depends (see below).

If you want a pot roast for dinner, the cross rib is a very good choice, maybe even the best choice for a quality pot roast. The cross rib can be found on sale at decent prices. The boneless chuck is sometimes much cheaper though, and second best is sometimes better if it means saving lots of money, and sometimes you can. The cross rib is also a very good oven

Cross Rib Roast

roast. If you plan on cooking a cross rib as an oven roast, you can replace it with top-round, rump, or sirloin tip roasts on sale, with very good results.

Heel of Round Roast:

Not very common anymore.

The heel of round is the end piece of the round after the full-cut round steaks have been cut away. It is an okay roast when trimmed, but it is more trouble than it is worth for most butchers. The heel is mostly used for stew meat, cube steak, or very lean ground beef. A cross rib or rump roast would be a good replacement and can be found on sale at reasonable prices.

Top Blade Roast or Flatiron Roast:

Money-saving alternatives: when on sale, boneless chuck roast and cross rib roast.

The top blade roast is also called a flatiron. The flatiron is a very flavorful cut that comes off the side of the whole cross rib. It has nice marbling, which gives it flavor, and it is fairly tender. When cooked as a pot roast, it has no equal. If you want a good pot roast, ask the butcher how much a flatiron or top blade roast is. You should be able to get one for the same price as a cross rib, so watch for a cross rib ad. If the price is right (the same ad price as a cross rib or rump roast), buy it.
Note: The first five inches of the flatiron when sliced thin and fried quickly, make outstanding steak sandwiches.

Ribs

Short Ribs:

Money-saving alternative: Who cares? Bring on the ribs! That is always my first emotional response to ribs. There are alternatives, however. See below.

I know a lot of you love short ribs, as I do, and will pay almost any price for them. I know, I've been selling them without any problem for years. Short ribs are very expensive, especially when you consider that half of what you get is bone and fat. There is good news, however. You don't have to spend all that money to enjoy ribs. The flatiron makes good ribs, too, as do boneless chuck flat strips. You can often find boneless country-style ribs cut from the flatiron or the boneless chuck flat strips for less than short ribs. Be careful, though; there are other cuts of beef used for boneless ribs that are not nearly as good as the flatiron or the chuck flat strips. Have your butcher help you with your selection. Ask him for the boneless country ribs made from the flatiron or the boneless chuck flat strips. Then pick out the ones with the most marbling (ribs are not a diet food). If you want good beef country ribs, then you want at the very least somewhat fatty ribs.

Flanken-Style Short Ribs:

Money-saving alternatives: back ribs, flatiron, or chuck flat strips.

Flanken-style ribs are thin-sliced (about three quarters of an inch) crosscut short ribs. Back ribs, although not as meaty, can be cut the same way for less money. The boneless flatiron or the chuck flat strip can be sliced thin and prepared the same way as the flanken-style rib as well, for a lot less money when you factor in the fact that they are all meat.

Boneless Chuck Flat Strips:

Money-saving alternative: none, see below.

The boneless chuck flat strip may be called something else in your area. It has lots of heavy marble and it cooks nice and juicy on the barbecue. It's not the most tender cut, but it's plenty tender enough and usually fairly inexpensive. I love it and I think most of you with your own teeth will, too. It is usually priced similar to boneless chuck roast and is a great value.

Boneless Beef Country-Style Ribs:

Money-saving alternatives: cross rib roast, chuck roast.

The best beef bone-less country-style ribs are made from the flatiron or the boneless chuck flat

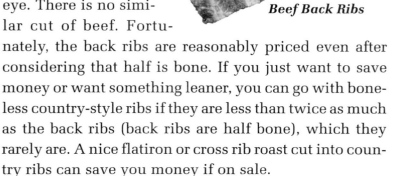

Beef Country Ribs, Flatiron Steaks, or Top Blade Steaks

strip and are often reasonably priced, but you can still save money by cutting up a cross rib roast or a boneless chuck roast that is on sale. Ask the butcher for help.

Beef Back Ribs:

Money-saving alternative: none, unless you want to settle for something leaner and less tasty.

Back ribs are the portion of the rib that is peeled away from the prime rib or rib eye. There is no simi-lar cut of beef. Fortu-

Beef Back Ribs

nately, the back ribs are reasonably priced even after considering that half is bone. If you just want to save money or want something leaner, you can go with bone-less country-style ribs if they are less than twice as much as the back ribs (back ribs are half bone), which they rarely are. A nice flatiron or cross rib roast cut into coun-try ribs can save you money if on sale.

MISCELLANEOUS CUTS

Cube Steaks:

Money-saving alternatives: top-round London broil, rump roast, cross rib roast, round steak, or any lean piece of meat.

Cube steaks make great chicken fried steaks and are made from lean pieces of trim generated from the day's

Beef Cube Steak

cutting. Any lean piece of meat will make good cube steaks. Simply find the leanest and the cheapest cut of meat in the meat case and ask the butcher to make cube steaks out of it. Chuck roasts and chuck steaks, as a rule, do not make very good cube steaks because of the excessive seams of fat. (See round steaks, page 22.)

Beef for Stir Fry:

Money-saving alternatives: top-round London broil, top-round roast or steak, round steak, sirloin tip roast or steak, or top sirloin when on sale.

Any of the above cuts will make good stir fry. Find the cheapest. It should be about half the price of premade beef strips for stir fry. Ask the butcher to cut your selection into stir fry strips, or take it home and cut it yourself. It's easy. Slice meat into half-inch slices and then slice again into strips.

Beef for Stew:

Money-saving alternatives: chuck roast, rump roast, cross rib roast, round steak, brisket, flatiron, chuck flat strip.

Stew meat is made from the trim that is left over from the day's cuttings. Even when stew meat is on sale, it may not be as cheap as many other cuts. Boneless chuck roasts and round steaks on sale will be cheaper, sometimes a lot cheaper. Find the cheapest and the leanest cut of meat and cut into cubes for stew or ask the butcher for his assistance. Now having said all that, the best meat for stew, in my humble opinion, comes from the brisket, flatiron, or the chuck flat strip. These three cuts should cost you less than the stew meat in the counter but may not be the best deal you can find. They will however be the best stew meat you will find.

Brisket:

Money-saving alternative: boneless chuck roast on sale.

Boneless Beef Brisket

Brisket, if not prepared properly, is the toughest cut of beef. It is also the cheapest. The whole brisket in the bag is very cheap. Brisket, with a little know-how, is outstanding barbecued, broiled, or as a pot roast. Boneless chuck roast on sale may be cheaper but is only a substitute if you are making a pot roast.

Corned Beef Brisket:

Money-saving alternative: none.

There is no substitute for corned beef brisket as far as saving money goes. The bottom round is also used for corned beef but will cost you quite a bit more. To save money, buy your corned beef the week of St. Patrick's Day. You will not find a better price all year, so fill your freezer and save. One note of caution: Watch out for the point cuts; they can be quite fatty. (The point cut is often the leader item for St. Patrick's Day.) You will find them especially cheap, with all the extra fat, but they're not necessarily the best buy. The flat cuts are nice and lean and may be the better value. Look them over closely; factor in the waste from the point cuts before making your purchase.

Beef Shank:

Money-saving alternatives: for soup or stew, a meaty soup bone or beef neck bones; for braised shanks, none.

Beef shanks are way overpriced if you simply want to make soup or stew. You can't beat some nice braised beef shanks, however, and there is no known substitute that will save you money. If you are making a soup or stew that calls for beef shanks, try a couple of nice marrow bone slices and some stew meat or a chunk of boneless chuck roast on sale, and cut it into stew meat.

Oxtail

Money-saving alternative: none.

There is nothing quite like the oxtail for making a nice, rich, dark broth. Oxtails are rather expensive at the supermarkets, but you can often find them much cheaper at your local custom meat shops and small meatpacking plants.

Beef Tongue:

Money-saving alternative: pork tongue.

Beef tongues only come one per animal, so they command a premium price at the supermarket. Local custom meat shops and small packing plants may have beef tongue for a lot less. Also, pork tongue is a very good substitute. If you have trouble finding pork tongue, try wholesale or custom meat plants.

Beef for Kabobs:

Money-saving alternatives: top sirloin, sirloin tip, petite sirloin.

©iStockphoto.com/Eva Serrabassa
Beef Kabobs

Beef kabobs in the meat case are going to cost you. You are much better off making your own. The best kabobs are made from the top sirloin, sirloin tip, or petite sirloin. Go with whatever is cheaper. Cut kabobs to your own specifications.

Breakfast Steak:

Money-saving alternatives: solid side of the sirloin tip sliced thin, top sirloin sliced thin, eye of round sliced thin, or the first four inches of the flatiron sliced thin.

Breakfast steaks are usually thin-sliced sirloin tip from the solid or silver side. They are expensive little steaks and can be replaced very nicely for less money with thin-cut top sirloin; or ask the butcher for a roast from the solid side of the sirloin tip and ask him to slice it into one-half-inch-thick breakfast steaks. You should save at least a couple of bucks a pound this way. Watch for eye of round roasts on sale, and have the butcher slice one thin for you. My favorite steak for breakfast is the flatiron sliced thin. The first three or four inches make the best breakfast steaks.

GROUND BEEF

Ground Sirloin:

Money-saving alternatives: sirloin tip roast, petite sirloin, top sirloin whole in the bag.

You can have ground sirloin for less than the regular price by asking the butcher to grind either a sirloin tip roast or petite sirloin

Ground Sirloin

steaks when they are on sale. If you want ground sirloin even cheaper, you will have to wait for a really hot whole top sirloin "in the bag" sale. When one comes along, pick out a nice lean one from the case and ask the butcher to grind it for you.

Extra Lean or Ground Round:

Money-saving alternatives: round steak, London broil, rump roast.

Round steaks on sale make great extra lean hamburger, as do rump roasts and London broils. Next time one of them is on sale, ask the butcher to grind some for you. Whenever you have the butcher grind something special for you, you will more than likely lose about half a pound of your product in the head of the grinder so make sure you grind enough product to make it worth your while. You can save a fair bit of money this way and get very good-quality hamburger. Fat content should be less than ten percent.

Lean Ground Beef or Ground Chuck:

Money-saving alternatives: boneless chuck roasts, cross rib roasts.

Boneless chuck or cross rib roasts make outstanding hamburger. Watch the ads and have the butcher grind some for you. The fat content will be more like extra lean than lean (about ten percent).

Regular Ground Beef:

Money-saving alternative: boneless chuck roasts.

Regular ground beef is 27 to 30 percent fat and usually priced to sell. However, you should be able to find boneless chuck roasts on sale for about the same price. Have the butcher grind some up for you. You may not save much, if any, money, but you will get a lot better product. Just about any cut of beef in the counter, when ground, will definitely make leaner and nicer ground beef than the regular hamburger.

CHOPS AND STEAKS

Loin Chop Bone-In Center Cut:

Money-saving alternatives: when on sale, boneless loin chops and boneless sirloin chops.

The bone-in loin chop is a pork T-bone. It has a New York cut on top, which is a boneless loin chop when the bone is removed, and the filet or tenderloin on the bottom. Boneless sirloin chops are cheaper than the bone-in center cut loin chops in most stores. The boneless sirloin, although not as pretty as the loin chop, is of similar

Center Cut Loin Chops Bone-In

quality. The boneless sirloin chop is a steal compared with the bone-in loin chop. Also, if you watch the ads, you can occasionally find boneless center cut loin chops for less money than the bone-in loin chops.

Rib Chop Bone-In Center Cut:

Money-saving alternatives: when on sale, boneless loin chops and boneless sirloin chops.

Rib chops are the same as loin chops except they do not have a tenderloin on one side of the bone. If the rib chop were beef, it would be called a rib steak, which comes from the prime rib. Boneless sirloin chops are similar in quality and are cheaper and boneless. Also, boneless loin chops are occasionally on sale for less than the rib chop.

Blade Chop Rib End and Bone-In Sirloin Chops:

Money-saving alternatives: boneless sirloin chops on sale, quarter loin or assorted chops on sale.

The bone-in sirloin chops and the rib end blade chops are found together in packages called quarter loin chops or assorted chops. They will sometimes be on sale this way at decent prices. However, the boneless sirloin is on sale quite often for the same or perhaps a little more than the assorted and quarter loin chops. The boneless sirloin does not have the waste of the bone-in chops and is usually the better buy. Figure the loss from the bone to be about 25 percent.

Assorted Chops, Quarter Loin Chops:

Money-saving alternatives: boneless sirloin and sometimes boneless loin chops.

The assorted chops are an assortment of rib, loin, blade, and sirloin chops or sometimes just the end chops, sirloin, and blade. This is the meat department's way of getting rid of the slow-moving end chops. Sometimes they are on sale cheap and sometimes not so cheap. When they are not so cheap, the boneless sirloin chop could be the better deal; when boneless loin chops are really hot, even they can sometimes be the better deal. Always consider the loss of bone and fat in your computations (about 25 percent).

Boneless Loin Chop:

Money-saving alternatives: sirloin chop, whole boneless loin "in the bag."

Wholesalers have been pumping out boneless pork loins with a passion over the past several years, and they keep getting cheaper. If you want a cheap pork chop, the boneless sir-

Boneless Loin Chops

loin is often the best deal. However, sometimes whole boneless pork loins (where boneless pork loin chops come from) are on sale even cheaper. If you can find boneless loins at the right price, you can either ask the butcher to cut them for you or take them home and slice them up yourself and save.

Boneless Sirloin Chops:

Money-saving alternative: pork shoulder blade steak.

Boneless sirloin chops are just about the best value of all the pork chops, especially when they are on sale, which they often are. The only thing cheaper might be assorted chops on sale—but they have a lot of bone—or a nice pork steak. It is not a chop, but it's still good and cheap at that (see pork shoulder blade steak).

Pork Shoulder Blade Steak:

Money-saving alternative: pork shoulder butt roast.

The pork shoulder butt blade steak, or simply the pork steak, is a tasty piece of pork that is quite often on sale. To get the best deal, though, wait until pork shoulder butt roasts are on sale (that is where the pork steak comes from). The butt roast at times is the cheapest cut of meat there is. When you see it advertised dirt cheap, ask the butcher to cut a butt or two into steaks. Cheap and good.

Pork Cube Steak:

Money-saving alternatives: pork shoulder butt roast, sirloin chops.

Pork cube steaks are made from what's left over after cutting the day's pork lineup. To save lots of money, buy a pork shoulder butt roast when it is on sale and have the butcher trim it up and make cube steaks from it. Part of the butt can be used for cube steaks, the other part for a roast, steaks, country-style ribs, or whatever you want.

Pork Cube Steaks

Pork Cutlets:

Money-saving alternatives: sliced boneless leg, boneless sirloin chops.

Pork cutlets are slices of lean pork that some butchers peel off of fresh picnics and other cheap cuts to boost profits. However, you do not have to fall victim to their merchandising. You can use boneless sirloin chops if you need cutlets. They are often on sale quite cheap. Ask the butcher to cut some boneless sirloin to your specifications or grab a fresh boneless leg roast, if the price is right, and have the butcher cut it into cutlets.

Whole Pork Loin Bone-In Sliced:

Money-saving alternatives: sometimes whole pork loin, assorted or quarter loin chops, boneless sirloin chops.

Sometimes whole bone-in pork loins go on sale; and when they do, they are sometimes a pretty good value. The bone-in loins can have up to 35 percent waste in the form of fat and bone (something to consider). Also, the presliced pork loins may not be a true whole pork loin. Oftentimes the butcher will "steal" a few center chops from each loin (a completely acceptable practice within the industry, one that will enthusiastically be denied by all but the most honest of butchers, like myself). The whole boneless pork loins, when on sale, may be a better value after considering the waste from the bone-in loins. The quarter loin pork chops or the assorted pork chops when on sale may be the better value as well. The quarter loin pork chops are supposed to be one fourth of a pork loin sliced into chops (they rarely are; usually the center chops are missing). The assorted pork chops are pretty much the same in most stores, just a different name. Watch for the whole boneless loins to go on sale, and you will get good quality for about as much as the cheap chops, if you are patient. The boneless sirloin chop has no waste and is often on sale at reasonable prices, making it the best buy.

Half Loin Bone-In:

Money-saving alternatives: quarter loin chops, assorted chops, boneless sirloin, whole boneless pork loins.

The half loin is supposed to be one half of the pork loin. There is the rib half and the loin half. Either half may not be a very good buy unless on sale for about the same price as you would find quarter loin or assorted chops. The boneless sirloin chop can be on sale for a little more than you might find assorted chops or half loins but, considering they are lean and boneless, they are almost always the better value. Sometimes the whole boneless pork loins on sale can be the better deal. Do the math. Bone-in loins will have 25 to 35 percent fat and bone.

ROASTS

Loin Roast Bone-In and Boneless:

Money-saving alternatives: whole boneless pork loin, boneless pork leg roast.

Pork loin roast bone-in or boneless can be expensive. They are the same roast, only one has a bone and the other doesn't. A whole boneless pork loin,

Boneless Loin Roast

when on sale, is a better bargain. The boneless pork leg is lean and nice and cheaper than the bone-in roast, sometimes making it an even better deal than the boneless pork loin. As always, watch the ads.

Sirloin Roast Bone-In:

Money-saving alternatives: boneless pork leg, boneless pork loin roast, whole boneless pork loin on sale, and boneless sirloin roast.

The bone-in sirloin roast is a very good roast, but almost half of it is bone, and it is hard to carve. Boneless sirloin roasts are small but very good with no waste.

They can be found on sale whenever the boneless sirloin chops are on sale. Ask the butcher if you do not see them. Boneless loin roasts are often cheaper than the bone-in sirloin roast, and without the waste. Boneless pork leg makes a nice roast, too, and should save you money.

Sirloin Roast Boneless:

Money-saving alternatives: boneless pork loin roast, boneless pork leg roast.

The boneless pork sirloin roast is a very nice, lean, and tender roast that is quite often on sale at a very good price. However, boneless pork loins in the bag are even cheaper at times and are great roasts and will make terrific boneless chops. The boneless leg roast may be competitively priced and make a nice substitute for the boneless sirloin roast as well.

Shoulder Blade Butt Roast:

Money-saving alternative: none (read on).

The butt roast is a very nice roast. It can be used as an oven roast or a pot roast and is often found on sale dirt cheap. The butt roast, when on sale, should be priced lower than the rock-bottom sale price of any other cut of beef or pork (except fresh picnics). When you find a sale, stock up. These make a great hamburger substitute for less than half the price of ground beef.

Fresh Shoulder Picnic Roast:

Money-saving alternatives: butt roast, sometimes boneless pork leg.

The shoulder roast or fresh picnic roast is usually smoked, but you can find fresh uncured shoulder roasts in most supermarket meat cases. They are often priced dirt cheap, even cheaper than pork shoulder butts, but they are not a better value. The pork shoulder roast has up to an inch of fat along with several ounces of rind and a big bone (up to 50 percent waste). The pork butt can be priced 30 percent more and will still be a better deal. Also, the boneless pork leg may be a better value when on sale. Always factor in the amount of loss from fat and bone before making your selection.

Pork Leg Roast Bone-In:

Money-saving alternative: boneless leg roast, bone-less sirloin roast.

Boneless pork leg roasts are often sold at reasonable prices. They are nice and lean without the excess fat, rind, and bone of the bone-in leg roast. Most whole pork legs may contain up to 30 percent or more fat, bone, and rind. Boneless sirloin roasts on sale are often cheaper than the boneless leg and make a very nice roast.

Pork Leg Boneless:

Money-saving alternative: boneless sirloin roast.

Boneless sirloin roasts are small but very tender and can be found on sale quite often for less than what a boneless leg might cost.

Boneless Pork Leg Roast

Rib Roast Center Cut:

Money-saving alternatives: boneless pork leg roast, boneless pork loin roast, whole boneless pork loin, boneless sirloin roast.

The center cut rib roast is from the loin and is a very nice roast. The boneless pork leg is also a very nice roast and it is cheaper, especially when it is on sale. Also, the boneless pork loin roast and the whole boneless pork loin may be priced less when on sale. The boneless sirloin is kind of small but very lean and tender and is quite often on sale cheap. About 20 to 25 percent of the center cut rib roast is bone, so be sure to factor that in before making your purchase.

Rib Roast Blade End:

Money-saving alternative: shoulder blade butt roast.

The blade end rib roast has lots of bone and fat. It is usually used for country-style ribs or chops. A nice butt roast is cheaper and just as good, if not better.

Tenderloin Roast:

Money-saving alternative: boneless loin roast.

The tenderloin is the filet mignon of pork. It is very tender and fairly small. Three or more tied together make a very nice roast, or they can be barbecued and sliced thin for Chinese dishes. The boneless pork loin can be found on sale for less than the tenderloin and can be used in the same way.

Ribs

Spareribs:

Money-saving alternatives: country-style ribs, pork shoulder butt roast.

There is nothing quite like barbecued ribs. However, they can be expensive, especially when you take into account that at least half is fat and bone. If you want to save money, there is an alternative. Country-style ribs are fairly lean compared with spareribs and

Secret Sauce recipe page 98

meatier. They are also cheaper, sometimes a lot cheaper when on sale. An even cheaper alternative for spareribs is the pork shoulder butt roast. This is the cut that country-style ribs are cut from. Next time you see pork butts on sale, have the butcher cut one into country-style ribs and save a bundle.

Baby Back Ribs:

Money-saving alternatives: spareribs, country-style ribs.

Most folks who want

Baby Back Ribs

baby back ribs probably do not want country-style ribs,

even though they are cheaper and meatier. But if you just have to have some real ribs, there is nothing wrong with spareribs. To tell you the truth, I can't tell the difference between spareribs and baby back ribs, except spareribs are meatier. They are both juicy and tender when prepared properly. So go with the spareribs and save.

Country-Style Ribs:

Money-saving alternative: butt roast.

Shoulder Cut (butt) Boneless Country Style Ribs

Country-style ribs are cut from either the blade end of the loin or the butt roast. To save money, watch for pork shoulder blade butt roasts on sale. Pick out a nice one, and ask the butcher to cut it into country-style ribs. You will save a bundle.

Pork Riblets:

Money-saving alternative: spareribs.

Riblets are cross cut ribs usually off the loin (baby back rib). The butcher cuts them from the loin to square it up before cutting pork chops. Either the baby back ribs or the spareribs will make good riblets, but the spareribs will be cheaper.

MISCELLANEOUS

Breakfast Sausage Bulk:

Money-saving alternative: pork shoulder blade butt roast.

Where sausage is concerned, you are at the mercy of the butcher unless you don't mind making your own. When pork butts are on sale, ask the butcher to grind one or more for you. Then take it home and mix in sausage seasoning purchased from a custom meat processing plant or retail meat shop, or experiment with your own seasonings. Basic sausage ingredients usually include a selection of the following: Salt, sugar, paprika, onion powder, garlic powder, sage, cayenne pepper, and MSG.

Italian Sausage Bulk:

Money-saving alternative: pork shoulder blade butt roast.

Italian sausage can cost you much more than what you need to pay. When you find a nice pork butt roast ad, ask the butcher to grind one or two for you. Then purchase some Italian sausage seasoning. If your butcher does not have any, call one of the custom meat or retail butcher shops in your area. You will save plenty.

Ground Pork:

Money-saving alternative: pork shoulder butt roast.

When butt roasts are on sale, they can be dirt cheap. They also make very nice and fairly lean ground pork and sausage. Select a nice butt roast from the case, and have the butcher grind it for you. It makes great hamburgers and can be used as a cheap but tasty substitute for ground beef.

Pork Kabobs:

Money-saving alternative: boneless sirloin chops.

If you want pork kabobs, find some boneless sirloin chops on sale and ask the butcher to cut some to your desired thickness. Then take them home and cut them into kabobs. You'll save a bundle!

©iStockphoto.com/Eva Serrabassa

(Most kabobs are one-inch square or larger.)

LAMB AND VEAL

Lamb:

Money-saving alternative: see below.

The best thing you can do to save money on lamb purchases is either watch the ads or shop for lamb in a store that is part of a major supermarket chain but located in a blue-collar neighborhood. Most major supermarkets have a meat counter schematic that is the same throughout the  chain. In a blue-collar meat and potatoes kind of neighborhood, lamb is not a regular part of the diet, but the local supermarket still has to carry a lamb lineup. In these types of stores, you may find legs of lamb and the like reduced to sell. I have worked in several stores just like this and have been eating lamb (and saving lots of money) ever since. Ask the butcher if the store ever reduces lamb and when to look for it. Another alternative is to buy a lamb from the farmer and have it processed at a local custom meat plant. Be aware that you will lose more than 50 percent from the processing.

©iStockphoto.com/Norma Cornes

Veal:

Money-saving alternative: for some applications, boneless pork can be substituted.

Veal can be very expensive. To save money, watch the ads and the reduced bins. Like lamb, you can find veal at reduced prices in some large supermarkets located in blue- collar neighborhoods (see Lamb).

Veal Scaloppini:

Money-saving alternatives: boneless leg of pork, boneless pork sirloin.

Thin Slices of Pork for Veal Scaloppini Substitute

Lean leg of pork or boneless pork sirloin sliced thin can be used as a substitute for veal scaloppini. The color is very similar and the taste is very mild. You will save a lot of money. Ask the butcher to slice a boneless leg or some boneless sirloin very thin for you. Go with the one that is cheaper.

Veal Parmesan:

Money-saving alternatives: pork cube steaks, boneless pork sirloin.

Pork made into cube steaks can be used as a substitute for veal parmesan. The pork cube steaks made from boneless sirloin or leg slices are very mild in flavor and make a nice cheap substitute. Ask the butcher to make cube steaks out of boneless pork sirloin when you see it on sale.

CHICKEN

Whole Fryers:

Money-saving alternative: sometimes fryer parts (see below).

When on sale, whole fryers are a great value. However, chicken hindquarters (drumstick, thigh, and part of the back) are often advertised at ridiculously low prices. If you like dark meat and want to save a lot of money, the hindquarter  is for you. Sometimes the fryer parts are on sale cheaper than the whole fryers. Even bone-in breasts are at times priced quite low. Watch the ads.

Breast Bone-In:

Money-saving alternative: boneless breast on sale.

Boneless breasts are on sale all the time at really good prices. Around 30 percent of the bone-in breast is skin and bone. Bone-in breasts will often be priced cheaper, but if you figure in the waste the boneless breasts are often the better deal.

Whole Cut-Up Fryer:

Money-saving alternatives: whole fryer, individual parts if on sale.

If you watch the ads you can sometimes purchase individual fryer parts for less than a whole cut-up chicken. However, it is best to buy a whole fryer when it is on sale and cut it up yourself.

Fryer Parts:

Money-saving alternatives: whole fryer, hindquarters.

Cut your own parts from whole fryers or buy fryer hindquarters on sale. The money you save on hindquarters may allow you to purchase a breast or two and still save. Also, fryer parts themselves are often on sale and very cheap.

Roasting Chicken:

Money-saving alternative: whole fryer.

The roasting chicken is nothing more than a large fryer. We used to take the largest fryers and wrap them up separately and price them 30 cents a pound or so higher than the whole fryers. Today the wholesale processors package the largest fryers as roasters before they get to the store. If you do not need a roaster quite as large as the ones being offered, grab a fryer and save.

Stewing Hen:

Money-saving alternatives: whole fryer, hindquarters.

This is one of those "gotcha" items. A stewing hen is a stewing hen and outside of maybe a stewing rooster, which I haven't seen in a retail market in years, there is no other way to get that rich chicken flavor for your soups and stews. The frying chicken is young and does not have the full flavor of the old hens. But if saving money counts (and it always has for me), you can save by purchasing hindquarters or whole fryers for your chicken and dumplings.

TIPS

1. Just because something is on sale doesn't mean you are getting a deal. Watch the prices, and become a knowledgeable shopper.

2. Beware of "Buy One Get One Free" ads. You never get anything for free. This is just another way to get you into the store. Oftentimes, if you do the math, you will find that the deal is not as good as it may seem.

3. Do not buy roasting chickens at a higher price than whole fryers. They are large fryers in disguise.

4. Fresh beef that has turned dark and has been reduced to sell can save you some considerable money. Beef turns dark rather quickly once it is exposed to the atmosphere, and color is not an accurate indicator of freshness. Besides, good beef has been aged at least 10 to 14 days anyway.

5. The larger the whole turkey or chicken, the better the yield. This means more meat vs. bones and skin, giving you more bite for the buck.

6. Do not buy stew meat. Look for round steak or chuck roasts on sale, and either take it home and cut it up or ask the butcher to do it for you. You will save a bundle.

7. Do not buy ground beef. Wait until round steaks, chuck roasts or steaks, or any other cheap cuts are on sale, and have the butcher grind them for you. The quality will be great and, if you buy right, so will the savings.

8. Veal for veal parmesan, scaloppini, and other dishes can be very expensive, but there is an alternative. Pork sirloin is cheap and almost the same color, mild in flavor and can make a good cheap substitute.

9. Many supermarket meat departments sell "yesterday's grind" (hamburger) at reduced prices. Usually the reduced grind is put out first thing in the morning. There is nothing wrong with it, and you can save quite a bit of money.

10. Do not buy any piece of meat already tenderized. Find the cut you want, and then ask the butcher to tenderize it for you and save.

11. Remember that all cuts of meat come from a larger and less expensive cut. Learn all you can about what comes from where, and you will save money.

12. Never ask for small amounts of meat to be ground special. One-half to three-fourths of a pound of meat will remain in the head of the grinder.

13. Always slice the meat across the grain. The grain will appear as lines all going for the most part in the same direction. Find the lines and cut across them.

14. Be nice to your butcher. A little kindness goes a long way.

INDEX

GLOSSARY

Breakfast Steak: a steak or chop sliced thin for quick frying.

Barbecue: a method of cooking that usually involves a zesty tomato-based sauce and a smoky enclosed cooking atmosphere.

Broiling: a form of cooking using the top element of the oven at an extremely high temperature.

Carcass: the entire body of the slaughtered animal.

Chicken Fry: preparing a tenderized steak as you would fried chicken. Dip a tenderized piece of meat in egg or milk, and cover with seasoned flour or some type of breading, and fry in grease until brown.

Choice: a grade given to beef that meets certain high standards such as marbling and confirmation. Second only to "prime" in quality.

Chuck: the shoulder section of the front quarter.

Country-Style: usually pertains to boneless beef or pork ribs. Boneless meat cut into strips for barbecue.

Cross Cut: to cut across instead of lengthwise as in flanken-style ribs.

Cured: meat that has been preserved with salt and usually some chemicals. This changes the texture, color, and flavor of such meats as ham and corned beef.

Cutlet: a slice of pork or veal that may or may not be tenderized for frying.

Eye: as in rib eye or round eye. It is the center of a cut of beef.

Filet Mignon: the French term for beef tenderloin.

Full-Cut: the whole cut as in a full-cut round steak (one whole slice of a round).

Fresh: a term used to describe pork that has not been cured and/or smoked. It is also used to describe any meat that has not been frozen.

Good: a grade of beef that is not of the quality of select, choice, or prime. Good beef is often young steers and heifers that just do not have the fat cover, marbling, or confirmation needed to grade higher.

Grade: used to describe what the quality of beef is—for example, prime, choice, select, good.

Grilling: a form of cooking that involves flames and smoke.

Lamb: young sheep, approximately six months old.

Leader Item: or loss leader, an item that is advertised and priced at a significantly reduced price to bring in customers.

Loin: the choicest section of the carcass, incorporating the strips of muscle on each side of the spine.

London Broil: used mainly for thick-cut top-round steaks. Also tenderized flank rolls have been known as London broil.

Marbling: flecks of fat in the meat.

Mutton: older sheep, usually ewes.

No Roll: usually beef that does not receive a grade. In years past, no roll was beef that was too good to grade "good" but would not be graded "choice" because it did not have the fat content. No roll beef is now graded out as "select" and is the preferred beef of most consumers because of its high quality without the extra fat of choice or prime.

Offal: the organs such as heart, kidneys, tripe, tongue, etc.

Oven Roast: a roast that can be cooked in the oven without moisture until reaching desired internal temperature. Best when cooked rare to medium.

Pot Roast: a cut of meat that is cooked in a sealed container with water for an extended amount of time to maximize tenderness.

Primal: a main section of the carcass from which individual portions are cut. The primal shortloin yields T-bone steak, New York steaks, and tenderloin steaks. The primal round yields round steaks, eye of round, bottom round, etc.

Prime: the highest grade of beef, determined by the fat content and confirmation. Prime has the most marbling of all the grades.

Prime Rib: a restaurant term for rib roast, standing rib roast, and rib eye roast bone-in, all of which are the same cut of beef.

Round: the big beefy leg and rump portion of the hindquarter.

Schematic: a set of guidelines or scheme for how the meat case is arranged. A place for everything and everything in its place.

Select: a grade of beef that is leaner than "choice" but of higher quality than "good". "Select" is the grade preferred by most consumers because of its consistent quality without the extra fat of the higher grades.

Shortloin: the primal that T-bone steaks are cut from and when boned out where New York and tenderloin steaks come from.

Swissing or Swiss: a form of cooking with liquid. Brown off a steak in a fry pan, add a gravy or sauce, and cook covered until tender.

Silver Side: the solid side section of the sirloin tip (where breakfast steaks and stir fry beef come from).

Smoked: when meat has been hung in a smoky environment until it takes on a smoky flavor. It does not mean that the meat has been cooked. A cold smoke does not reach a high enough temperature to be considered cooked. Normally the meat has been cured with salt and certain preservatives before smoking.

Trim: scraps of meat left after cutting and shaping the individual cuts. The trim is generally used for stew meat, cube steaks, or grinds (hamburger).

Tenderized: a term used for meat that has gone through the tenderizer machine. The machine has many small blades that cut into the meat, thereby breaking down the chewy fibers.

Veal: the meat from two- to three-month-old, milk-fed beef animals.

Whole and In the Bag: a primal cut, vacuum sealed as it comes from the wholesale processor. See Primal.

APPENDIX
Additional Articles and Recipes

Talking Turkey

What To Do with the Leftover Turkey

John's Own Turkey Enchiladas

Turkey Pot Pie "Bachelor Style"

Totally Awesome Chili

Cheap and Easy Meat Loaf

Marine Corps Railroad-Style Barbecue Sauce

Way Easy and Way Delectable Ribs

Tools of the Trade

Butcher Etiquette

TALKING TURKEY

Purchasing the right turkey at Thanksgiving can be a great opportunity to save money and get a good-quality product worthy of a holiday spread. Yes, it is true. You can do both. I am a butcher. For the past 31 Thanksgivings, shoppers have come to me for help in choosing just the right turkey for their holiday feast and, frankly, I'm getting a little tired of it. It's time to educate. It's time to talk turkey.

There are three main questions I am asked every year without fail. Where's the cold beer? Do you have fresh dip? and How do you fix buffalo wings? No, wait, sorry, those are the three most asked Super Bowl questions.

The three most commonly asked questions by consumers at Turkey Time are, Where are the turkeys? Maybe I'd better make it the four most commonly asked questions at Thanksgiving. How about we skip that one and go to the next #1 question?

Which brand is best? A very good question, you might think, if you hadn't heard it 16,000 times a year for the past 31 years. OK, in answer to this question, let's talk about what I like to refer to as The Best Turkey Myth. The best turkey, according to the majority of consumers, is the one they are most familiar with. This means the turkey with the best advertising campaign is the one that shoppers are inclined to purchase the most. Since advertising costs are high, the cost of the well-known name brand turkey will be also. Just because a turkey has a brand name that you recognize doesn't mean that it will be the best turkey. It just means that it is well known.

On the other hand, there are turkeys with all sorts of unfamiliar labels being used as holiday "leader" items. These are the Buy One Get One Free, or the buy $50 worth of groceries and get a turkey free, or the really down and dirty cheap turkeys-all used to lure the poor unsuspecting shopper into their store. These turkeys may have obscure brand names, but they are often the very same turkey as the well-known brand name turkeys. Many of the large turkey processors put several different labels on their turkeys. In fact, many large supermarket chains have their own brand name turkeys, which are quite often the very same turkey as the local big name brand turkey. These store brand turkeys are excellent turkeys and are quite often the stores' "leader" turkeys, meaning you can get them cheap.

There is no discernable difference in most brand names, so just go with the cheapest. I have always purchased the very cheapest birds for our family holiday, and they have been very good; I have sold tens of thousands of the same with the same consistent results.

The trick in choosing the right turkey is not in the brand name, which leads us to question #2. Which turkey is freshest? Or, how do I know if this turkey is fresh? Now before we go any further, let me make one thing perfectly clear. It's not our fault. Please do not get angry at the butcher if your fresh turkey is as hard as a rock. They come in that way. According to the people who make the laws of this great country, turkeys can be called fresh even though the moisture in the bird is frozen. You will find that if you press very firmly on the bird, the meat is not frozen. The turkey processors have it down to a science. They bring the temperature of the birds down to the very legal limit before sending them off to the store up to two weeks before Thanksgiving so that your fresh turkey will be nice and fresh for your holiday meal.

That's right, we receive our fresh turkeys almost a full two weeks before Thanksgiving! Now please do not overreact to this. The turkeys are in great shape and will serve you well. In the old days we used to get them a full three weeks early, and they were fine, too. It's just in answer to question #2, the freshest turkey is really a frozen turkey. Frozen turkeys are quick frozen immediately after butchering. Also, the freezing process has no noticeable effect on the quality of the bird. The frozen turkey will generally be much cheaper than the fresh turkey.

OK, so now we know that fresh turkeys are not the freshest turkeys available and not to worry about the brand name. And now for the most important question of the three most commonly asked questions, How do we choose the right turkey? Actually it's quite simple. Select the plumpest bird in your desired weight class (not your own personal weight class but the weight of the turkey). For instance, you want a 15-pounder. Look over all the 15-pounders and select the plumpest. Some 15-pounders will be slim and some will be fat. Some turkeys are flat chested and some are kind of bony. Choose the most rounded and plump turkey. It's that easy. If a bird is skinny, it could mean it wasn't a very healthy bird and might be tough and dry. Also, the bone and fat will cost you just as much as the meat, so more meat/less waste is better. Another thing to know is that the larger the turkey, the better the good usable meat to bone and fat ratio. Bigger sometimes is better.

One other question gets asked a lot. What is the difference between a tom and a hen turkey? Now if you're old enough to drive down to the local supermarket and purchase a turkey for Thanksgiving, you would think that you would know the answer to this question. The truth is, most folks don't. The turkey people who process all these millions of birds do not have time to do a thorough survey or give any kind of exam. What they do is separate the birds by their size. Most of the birds that are 16 pounds or more are usually called toms and all the 15-pounders and smaller are hens.

OK, let's go over what we have learned. In choosing a turkey, do not worry about getting a certain brand unless you own stock in the company. The freshest turkey is a frozen turkey. Pick the plumpest turkey you can find. Toms are big and hens are small. Another thing, turkeys can be a great value at Thanksgiving. It's a good time to fill your freezer. Don't buy $50 worth of groceries to get a free turkey unless you intend to do your shopping there, and do not purchase anything except what you need at the right price. Watch out for Buy One Get One Free ads. Do the math, and have a nice and thrifty holiday.

What To Do with the Leftover Turkey

Turkey leftovers are my favorite leftovers. Even before that golden bird is pulled from the oven, I'm thinking of all the yummy meals to come from all the leftover turkey. The second turkey meal is usually a lot like the first. We warm up the yams and stuffing, mashed potatoes, and gravy and a generous amount of turkey for another turkey feast that can't be beat. Then the next several meals we get creative. Turkey enchiladas are a Smith family favorite and generally the most requested leftover entrée.

I clear the kitchen of all children and/or spouses (or spouse as in my case-one is plenty). I need a lot of room when I do my culinary thing so I also clear some counter space as well. His and her napkin holders from Yellowstone Park and a Julia Child bobble head doll have no place on a man's counter when there is work to be done. Next, I break out all the ingredients needed, including the tools necessary for the job. Once everything is in place, I start chopping and ripping and boiling and sautéing and rolling and saucing and grating and spreading until the enchiladas are ready for the oven. They are truly scrumptious.

JOHN'S VERY OWN
TURKEY ENCHILADAS

2-3 lbs. leftover turkey meat

2-3 cups leftover turkey gravy and/or cream of chicken soup

1 large chopped onion

1-2 small cans chopped green chilies (optional)

1-2 lbs. grated cheddar cheese

1-2 15-ounce cans enchilada sauce

10-20 flour or corn tortillas

salt and pepper to taste

I know the recipe sounds a little vague. That's because I don't measure. Here's what you do. Take the leftover turkey and cut it up into about 1-inch chunks. Add just enough leftover gravy and/or cream of chicken soup straight from the can to the turkey to make it goopy.  Add salt and pepper to taste and warm up mixture, stirring gently. Do not overstir, or the turkey will shred. Sauté onions and add them and the chopped green chilies and 1 to 2 cups grated cheddar cheese. Next, spoon the goop into flour tortillas, roll 'em up, and fill up a large pan with them. It's OK to cram them in tight. If using corn tortillas, you will need to warm them in the fry pan to make them flexible. Next, take some more of the gravy and/or cream of chicken soup and add the enchilada sauce to it (about 50/50). Warm up mixture until it is thoroughly blended. Pour this mixture over enchiladas, smothering them all with a light but thorough covering. Add grated cheese over the top and bake for 45 minutes at 325°F. Serve on a bed of lettuce garnished with slices of avocado, sour cream, and your favorite salsa with some nice Spanish rice and refried beans on the side and (slobber, drool, swallow) you're gonna be in pig heaven.

TURKEY POT PIE "BACHELOR STYLE"

You know I wasn't always a member of the blissfully wed crowd. Oh no, many moons ago I was a strapping young single lad with places to go and fillies to see. I didn't have time to burn up in the kitchen. So if I wanted a hot home-cooked meal, I either had to go to Mom's, which wasn't a bad idea; or have one of my many female  friends fix me one, which was a bad idea; or cook one myself. So I learned to make do and with time being a factor I learned to take short cuts. I would take this packet of that and that can of this and next thing you know I had discovered some very tasty quick meals. Turkey pot pie "bachelor style" is one of the better ones.

2 cups leftover turkey cut into one-inch chunks

3 15-ounce cans mixed vegetables (peas, carrots, potatoes, etc.)

1 small chopped onion

2 cans cream of chicken soup

1 cup milk

salt and pepper to taste

2 frozen pie shells

Sauté chopped onion and mix with turkey chunks and cream of chicken soup and milk until it is the right consistency. Warm mixture in pan on top of stove, stirring gently so as not to shred turkey. Drain vegetables and add to mixture. Add salt and pepper to taste. Pour mixture into pie shell and top with other pie shell. You may want to thaw out the top shell some so it is flexible. Crimp down the sides, fork holes in the top, and bake in a 350°F oven for about 45 minutes or until golden brown and bubbly. Good enough for married folks, let alone desperate bachelors.

TOTALLY AWESOME CHILI

Like me, chili is cheap. You can go all out and spend as much money making chili as you want, but I'm here to tell you that is not necessary. You can make a great big pot of the stuff that will last for days for just a few dollars. The basic ingredients, beans and hamburger, are generally not going to break the bank. Plus, if you use my  easy to follow award-winning (that's right, first prize at our church's annual chili cook-off of 2001) recipe you, too, can save even more money and maybe even wow your friends. Of course, if you start winning your church chili contest every year, you will soon find out who your friends really are.

The secret to saving money making chili is spending as little as possible for the most expensive ingredient. Nice ground beef for chili can set you back some. You have several choices. You can purchase hamburger already to go, paying top dollar, or wait for a boneless chuck roast sale and ask the butcher to grind a roast or two for you. Chuck roasts make outstanding hamburger,

©iStockphoto.com/
Stephen Walls

and this will cut your costs—maybe in half.

Another money-saving alternative is ground turkey. The frozen rolls in the meat section of the freezer are the way to go. The frozen rolls are of good quality minus the frilly and fancy packaging and the big name of the fresh stuff. I have actually made chili from time to time with ground turkey with pretty good results.

My favorite money-saving alternative for making my award-winning chili is ground pork butts. Pork butts can be found on sale all the time dirt cheap. They make great tasting "hamburger." They have just the right fat content, perfect for chili. Next time you see pork butts on sale at that rock-bottom down and dirty price, scarf up a bunch of them and ask the butcher to grind them for you and fill up the freezer. Ground pork butts make great hamburger and can be used in just about any application that ground beef is used in. Experiment and save some money.

Also, don't use canned beans. They just aren't as good, and it's much cheaper to get some nice new dry beans. The chili powder can be expensive, too, so just go down to your local huge warehouse-type supermarket and get it in bulk for a whole lot less than what you'd pay for a fancy little shaker container.

Now just follow my cheap and easy award-winning chili recipe and be the envy of all your friends.

John's Awesome Way Good Cheap Chili

2 lbs. ground pork butts

2 lbs. dried (new-this year's) pinto beans

2 medium onions, chopped

1 large green bell pepper, chopped

1/2 cup pickled jalapeno peppers, chopped

1/4 cup flour (or so)

4 heaping tablespoons chili powder or so, to taste (I actually end up using quite a bit more)

2 tablespoons sugar or so to taste (the sugar is used to mellow the flavor, not make it sweet, so go easy)

1 cup Pace hot salsa

4 to 5 small cans tomato sauce

1-2 large cloves fresh garlic

1 teaspoon or so chopped red hot chili peppers (optional)

salt to taste

A few hours before dinner, put new pinto beans on to boil. Use just enough water to cook the beans. Do not make soup! If your beans are fresh, meaning less than a year old, they will get nice and tender in a few hours. If they are not new beans, they may never get tender. Brown the ground pork with onions, garlic, and peppers. Once meat is cooked, mix flour in thoroughly. Add tomato sauce and chili powder and simmer a few minutes. Mix meat mixture in with cooked beans and water, add remaining ingredients, bring to boil, and simmer for awhile. Make adjustments on seasonings to suit your taste. For thicker chili, tomato puree or a little tomato paste can be used with or in place of tomato sauce. You can see that this recipe is not an exact science. Just trust yourself, and may the force be with you.

CHEAP AND EASY MEAT LOAF

Why do we like meat loaf? Did you ever ask yourself that question? There are a lot of good compelling reasons for fixing a nice big meaty meat loaf. My guess is that somebody's mom somewhere decided to try and stretch the last little dab of hamburger by adding bread crumbs and such. Little did she know that her desperate little experiment would become so popular. Now many of us make meat loaf just because it's delicious. But did you know that you can still, even today in these prosperous post-depression modern times, save money by making a nice meat loaf? We can spend as much money as you and I want on nice tender steaks, and you've got your prime ribs and other high end-type roasts, but why should we if we don't have to? When it comes right down to it, there is nothing like a nice slab of money-saving meat loaf.

©iStockphoto.com/Kelly Cline

Of course, just like steaks and roasts, not all meat
loaf is created equal. I have had meat loaf as dry as the
Mojave desert in the middle of summer (sorry, Mom). I
have also had meat loaf that is so bland that after going
to bed I dreamed of eating hospital food and liking it.
There are lots of other meat loaf disasters, some of which
I can't talk about right now—at least not until the inves-
tigations have been completed.

Good meat loaf starts with good ground beef. You
can use the "all ready to go hamburger" in the meat
counter, but chances are you are spending too much for
too little. The prepackaged ground beef is generally made
from old cows with questionable vitality and heritage.
Even the ground beef made in the shop will have some
of that mystery meat mixed in with the shop trim. You
can, however, get outstanding quality and even save
money.

Next time you want to make a nice meat loaf, look
for boneless chuck roasts on sale. Usually you will find
some somewhere. Boneless chuck roasts on sale can be
as low as $1.69 a pound (sometimes more, sometimes
maybe even less). Grab a couple of nice ones from the
counter and hand them to the butcher and ask to have
them ground up. Ground chuck has the best flavor, and
it will be plenty lean. You now have in your possession
the best hamburger known to mankind, or at least to
me. You can grind filet mignon, but it won't have the
flavor of ground chuck. Now all you have to do is fol-

low my cheap and easy meat loaf recipe, save money, and thrill your friends.

Cheap and Easy Meat Loaf

1 1/2 pounds fresh ground chuck

1/2 pound pork breakfast sausage (the fatter and cheaper, the better)

1 medium onion, chopped

1/2 green bell pepper, chopped

1 celery stalk, chopped

2 cups dry bread crumbs or crushed crackers

3 eggs

1 level teaspoon salt

1/2 teaspoon pepper

1 clove garlic run through a garlic press

4 tablespoons watered down type Worcestershire sauce

Mix all ingredients well and mold into a loaf. Place in a pan with plenty of room. Bake at 325°F until internal temperature reaches 170°F or about an hour and a half. Some folks like to smother the meat loaf in ketchup about 15 minutes before pulling from the oven, or serve with brown gravy.

There you have it-cheap and easy, and good meat loaf.

MARINE CORPS RAILROAD-STYLE BARBECUE SAUCE

When I was a young cook in our nation's finest military establishment, we used to right a lot of wrongs come dinnertime with a special barbecue sauce. You see, most of the cooks responsible for fueling the world's elite fighting machine were not assigned to the galley because of any kind of culinary skill or disposition. In fact, most of us would have gladly traded our spatulas and aprons for an M-16 and a chance to pick up cigarette butts from 8 to 4, I mean zero 800 to ah, whatever, and then hit town on liberty until dawn like a real Marine. But nooo..., we of the grimy white T-shirts and soiled white cotton trousers and funny looking white cook hats had to get up at zero dark thirty every morning to fulfill our obligation to our fine country by slopping the, I mean feeding the, troops. So on account of the poor attitudes of some of the cooks toward this time-honored and important responsibility, many of the meals weren't fixed with the same care and love that, say, Mom, always seemed to use when fixing our food at home. In other words, the food sucked.

Of course, a few nasty comments did not bother us cooks; after all, we were tough, too. But after awhile things began to get more and more ugly at mealtime. The troops were very picky. They did not like our rendition of egg drop soup with chunks of gelatinized corn starch the size of softballs or the chocolate pudding with a rubbery top that Goodyear is still studying for a possible synthetic replacement for rubber or the stew that one of the cooks dropped a 25-pound bag of salt into. They especially hated it when we would serve dried-out roasts, which was only when we fixed roasts, which was several times a week, but we had good intentions. We just could not get into our brains the concept of breaking out the frozen meat the night before to thaw. So after we would throw several hundred pounds of frozen beef or pork roasts into our giant rotisserie ovens, with the heat turned up full blast to make sure they would reach the desired internal temperature in time for dinner, we decided that we needed to do something a little different before the troops began bringing their weapons to the mess hall.

Necessity is the mother of invention, and we needed to do something and quick to pacify several hundred of the Marine Corps' finest. So the next time we burned off several hundred pounds of roast meat, we decided that what we needed was a sauce to moisten things up a bit. Now some brown gravy would be nice, except for the fact that our gravy was rarely nice or even brown, for that matter. That is when we got the idea that maybe a barbecue sauce might be in order. At that time, the Marine Corps was not supplying us with any kind of canned or otherwise barbecue sauce, so we would have to make our own-scary thought, indeed.

Several of us men in white solemnly gathered around a large steam-jacketed kettle. After brainstorming for a painful moment or two, we decided to go with a ketchup base, for no real apparent reason. Into the large kettle went three gallons of ketchup. Next we deduced that barbecue sauce has to be sweet and have a bite, so we dumped in several bottles of Louisiana hot sauce and a couple of cans of molasses. Someone said that all barbecue sauces have vinegar for tang, so in went a 12-ounce bottle of apple cider vinegar. Then we just added whatever we thought would taste good on meat-garlic powder, onion powder, salt, pepper, MSG, etc., and guess what? It was terrific! This sauce may have been the first thing some of us ever made that actually tasted good. In fact, it was better than good-it was out &%$?)$# standing! (That's a military term for really good.)

I have been using this Marine Corps Railroad (railroad is a term used for winging it, cooking without a net, so to speak) Style Barbecue Sauce ever since, and it is still delicious. You can take a cheap tough cut of meat and, with a little of this special sauce and a roasting pan, turn it into a feast fit for the Corps.

Marine Corps Railroad-Style Barbecue Sauce

1 24-oz bottle ketchup

3-4 tablespoons molasses

4 tablespoons Worcestershire sauce

A couple of good shakes Tabasco sauce

2 tsp apple cider vinegar

1 tsp onion powder

1 tsp garlic powder

1/2 tsp MSG (optional)

1 tsp salt

1/2 tsp black pepper

All ingredients can and should be adjusted to suit your taste. This sauce turns out differently every time I make it, but it is always delicious.

Mix all ingredients, and pour liberally over and under your favorite cheap meat in roasting pan. Cover and cook at 275°F for 2-3 hours or until tender or slather it all over a big hunk of meat and throw it onto a hot grill turning and covering in sauce as it cooks.

My favorite cheap meat is country-style ribs cut from a pork butt on sale dirt cheap, of course. Good luck and "Semper Fi."

WAY EASY AND WAY DELECTABLE RIBS

You know that ribs are good—actually better than good, they are outstanding. The problem with ribs, though, is that they take time, too much time. I know guys who stand over their ribs for hours, basting and turning to get them just perfect, only to have a brother-in-law or neighbor come over right at the very moment you sit down to enjoy your labors and polish off an undesignated portion, leaving less for you.

From the moment you put those delectable slabs of meat on the grill, all slathered with your favorite secret barbecue concoction, the whole neighborhood is alerted by the wafts of drool-inducing smoke that oozes over their fences. You can't win. Being the kind and generous soul that you are, you know that there is no getting around having to share your ribs with some unworthy opportunist with a gluttonous appetite who just happens to come by right as you are sitting down for dinner. There is a solution.

While it is true that you cannot mask the wonderful aroma that exudes from the ribs as they cook, there is a way to cut back on your labors so as to make the whole sharing ordeal a lot less traumatic. Instead of standing for hours basting your ribs over a hot grill, try my little trick for easy and delectable ribs. The first thing I do is cut the ribs into 1- to 2-inch strips and then cut between the bones, making little individual riblets. You then take the little riblets and throw them in either an electric skillet or large roasting pan, depending on the amount of ribs you are fixing. Then pour your secret sauce liberally over and under the ribs, mixing thoroughly. Place the lid on the skillet or roasting pan a little askew to let the excess moisture evaporate. Cook at a very low temperature. You want to cook them as slowly as you can. Once the barbecue sauce has thickened into a reddish black bubbly goo and the ribs are melt-in-your-mouth tender, they are done. It may take about 2-1/2 to 3 hours or more. It still takes time, but you can be watching the game or something instead of standing over the grill; the smell will still alert the neighbors, but you could try closing all doors and windows to trap the smell. If that doesn't do the trick, turn off all the lights and pretend you're not home. It works for me.

TOOLS OF THE TRADE

For those of you who want to take your cheapness to the next level, this is the section for you. Up until now I've been recommending that you ask the butcher to do all the slicing and dicing and grinding for you, which is fine, except it really isn't practical or all that convenient if you re-ally want to take advantage of the sales and all the good deals that are out there for the informed meat monger. For example, say pork butts are on sale for 99 cents a pound. You may want to buy a hundred pounds of them. Do you want it all into ground pork or maybe some into sausage? Do you want some Italian sausage for making pizza and spaghetti or all into breakfast sausage? You might like some roasts and maybe you want some boneless country-style ribs to barbecue. How about some delicious pork cutlets breaded and fried then covered in cream of chicken soup, covered and baked until they are melt-in-your-mouth tender in your favorite roasting pan? There are a lot of things you can do with a pork butt. There are also a lot of things you can do with a bunch of boneless chuck roasts when on sale or round steaks or boneless pork loins, etc.

Don't limit yourself. If you have the proper tools at home, then you can buy whatever you want, fill the freezer with money-saving cheap meat, and then cut or grind it into any shape or form that suits your fancy. If you read carefully what the alternatives are for each cut of meat, you can figure out what it is you would like to stock up on and, with a little help from the butcher, you can easily figure out what to do with each cut.

So if you are serious, the first thing you will need is a decent cutting surface. I bet you thought I was going to say a sharp professional-type knife. A sharp knife is important, but if you do not have a proper cutting surface, your sharp expensive professional-type knife will soon be joining the other beat-up blunt instruments in your kitchen drawer. The cutting boards under the countertop that slide in and out actually work quite well for a cutting surface. You can purchase a nice cutting board, but make sure it is wood or that soft white semi plastic-type stuff that almost all butcher shops use and not one of those fancy hard formica-type cutting boards. Those are for looks only. If you draw the edge of your knife across the surface of your board and do not cut into it, it is too hard. A good cutting board will not dull your knife; a bad one will.

Now you are ready for a nice sharp knife. There are many brands that will do, but you may have a tough time finding one at a decent price. There are specialty stores where you can purchase a professional steak or boning knife at a premium. If you have gotten to the point where you are on a first-name basis with your butcher, ask him where he gets his knives and see if you can purchase a knife or two through him. He will be able to help you with your selection. I suggest an eight-inch steak knife. It is very versatile. It's small enough to do some boning, and it is large enough to slice through almost anything except maybe full-cut rounds. At work most of us use a ten-inch steak knife and a six-inch flex boner, but I love a nice sharp eight-inch. It is really easy to handle. As far as brands go, the Forschner is the most popular. It is made with nice hard steel and will last you a lifetime. However, I actually prefer the second rate-type knives like Atlanta sharp Tech, Hookeye, Safety Kleene, and others. The steel in these knives is just a tad bit softer, which makes it easier to keep sharp. I can go months without sharpening one of these knives by just using my smooth steel to straighten out the edge. The Forschner is a lot less forgiving. It takes a bit more skill to put and keep an edge on it. It is a good knife though and, of course, you will pay more for one.

Next you will need a way to keep your knife sharp. I have always used a smooth steel. A steel is a long cylindrical piece of stainless steel on a handle. A lot of people have rough steels, but I do not recommend them. More often than not, they will keep your knife dull by taking the edge off the knife rather than putting one on. All you need is to occasionally run your knife gently over a smooth steel to straighten out the edge.

If your knife gets to the point where a smooth steel

no longer works, it is time to use a stone. There are lots of stones available and the only one I recommend is the medium surface replacement stone for the three-in-one stone holder. That is what 99.9 percent of all butcher shops use. It is about ten inches long and about 2-1/2 to 3 inches wide. These work great and can be purchased from the same places that sell knives. You might find a nice stone in a holder, and that's fine, but you will probably spend more money than you need to for something you really won't use that often. To use the stone, place it sideways on a damp towel on the edge of your kitchen counter. Rub mineral oil liberally over the stone. Hold the handle of the knife in your slicing hand, and place your other hand on the back side of the tip of the knife and draw the blade from one side to the other against the edge. Make sure to draw the knife across the entire length of the stone, angling the knife at the same degree as the existing bevel of the knife. Draw the knife across the stone about 3 to 4 times on each side. If you do this correctly, that will be all that you will need to do. It's a little tricky to get just the right angle, so hang in there.

If you have purchased a nice sharp knife, I highly recommend a safety glove. I have gone for decades without one and my hands have hundreds of scars to show for it. Now I use one all the time. I can be taught! There are two main types of safety gloves—steel mesh and heavy duty fabric. I like the fabric glove because it is so much more comfortable and works great. You can purchase one of these gloves from any of the meat equipment suppliers. Your butcher can probably get you one as well.

Another item that is invaluable in the kitchen is a good heavy duty meat grinder. I just recently purchased the largest hand cranker I could find and it works great. However it takes a couple of strong arms to operate, one arm to hold it steady and another to crank. It can be bolted down to a secure surface which should make it easy enough for most people to operate. Be careful of the inexpensive electric grinders. Many of them just do not have much power and can't handle any large grinding job. You can find grinders online or in any kitchen or restaurant specialty store.

So now you are set. You've got a nice soft surface to cut on. You have a nice sharp knife. You have a smooth steel and a medium surface stone to keep your knife sharp and a safety glove to keep your hand from getting sliced and diced, and with a nice heavy duty grinder you can tackle any kind of meat processing job. Now you can get out there and save some serious dough.

Butcher Etiquette

For the most part, the meat cutters you run into will be nice enough, but most of them are quite busy, and making requests for extra slicing and dicing and grinding could put a strain on your relationship. To keep on the best of terms with your butcher, which is what you want to do if you are to truly get the best deals possible, here are a few tips.

1. Give your butcher plenty of time to take care of your order. Tell him you can pick it up whenever it is convenient for him. Try to avoid asking for special requests during peak shopping times.

2. Make sure that you always pick up your order in a timely manner. Never leave it longer than the appointed hour. This makes butchers nervous, and if you leave it too long they will reprocess it for the counter. Don't pick it up at all, and risk doing irreparable damage to your relationship.

3. To really butter up your butcher, always leave a nice comment on his helpfulness and professionalism as you go through the check stand. Tell the manager how happy you are with him. Some homemade cookies once in awhile won't hurt either.

There you have it. Three little rules to keep your butcher happy. Remember, a happy butcher is a helpful butcher, and chocolate chip cookies or snickerdoodles will be just fine.

ABOUT THE AUTHOR

After three years of slaving over hot grills and giant steam-jacketed kettles as a cook in the United States Marine Corps, author John Smith took a job in a small butcher shop. With broad shoulders and not a lot else going for him, he applied himself to the trade. The first few years, John worked in custom locker plants and small meatpacking houses learning to take the beef out in the pasture and get it ready for the skillet. Now, after some 31 years in the meat industry, he's done it all, from wholesale to retail and everything in between.

Also, somewhere along the way, John began to release a suppressed urge to express himself with the written word. John and his wife Vickie published a nationally distributed newsletter called *Ark Essentials*, dedicated to "emergency preparedness and provident living." It is this appreciation of provident living that has inspired John to share with any who will listen how to make a dollar stretch to its fullest when purchasing meat.

Another motivating factor in John's commitment to frugality is that he is the proud father of ten children.

Published by Ark Essentials, Inc.
P.O. Box 634
Ashton, ID 83420
www.arkessentialspublishing.com